Talking Hands

SEASONS

ESTACIONES

The Child's World

Published in the United States of America by The Child's World®
PO Box 326, Chanhassen, MN 55317-0326
800-599-READ
www.childsworld.com

Photo Credits: Brand X Pictures/Burke/Triolo Productions: 17, 19; Comstock: 3, 4, 8, 9, 10, 12, 20; Photodisc: cover (left), 1 (left), 2, 8, 13, 14–15, 21 (all); Photodisc/C Squared Studios: cover (right), 1 (right), 5, 6, 7, 16, 18–19, 22, 22–23; Photodisc/G. K. and Vikki Hart: 14; Stockbyte: 11.

The Child's World®: Mary Berendes, Publishing Director

Editorial Directions, Inc.: E. Russell Primm, Editorial Director; Katie Marsico and Elizabeth K. Martin, Associate Editors; Kathleen Petelinsek and E. Russell Primm, Photo Researchers

The Design Lab: Kathleen Petelinsek, design, and page production; Kari Thornborough, production assistant

LIBRARY OF CONGRESS CATALOGING-IN-PUBLICATION DATA
Petelinsek, Kathleen.
  Seasons = Estaciones / by Kathleen Petelinsek and E. Russell Primm; content advisers, Carmine L. Vozzolo and Kim Bianco Majeri.
    p. cm. — (Talking hands)
  Includes bibliographical references and index.
  English, Spanish, and American Sign Language.
  ISBN 1-59296-023-5 (lib. bdg. : alk. paper) 1. American Sign Language—Vocabulary—Juvenile literature. 2. Spanish language—Vocabulary—Juvenile literature. 3. Seasons—Juvenile literature. I. Title: Estaciones. II. Primm, E. Russell, 1958– III. Title.
  HV2476.P48 2005
  419'.7081—dc22
                                    2004000693

NOTE TO PARENTS AND EDUCATORS:
The understanding of any language begins with the acquisition of vocabulary, whether the language is spoken or manual. The books in the Talking Hands series provide readers, both young and old, with a first introduction to basic American Sign Language signs. Combining close photo cues and simple, but detailed, line illustration, children and adults alike can begin the process of learning American Sign Language. In addition to the English word and sign for that word, we have included the Spanish word. The addition of the Spanish word is a wonderful way to allow children to see multiple ways (English, Spanish, signed) to say the same word. This is also beneficial for Spanish-speaking families to learn the sign even though they may not know the English word for that object.

Let these books be an introduction to the world of American Sign Language. Most languages have regional dialects and multiple ways of expressing the same thought. This is also true for sign language. We have attempted to use the most common version of the signs for the words in this series. As with any language, the best way to learn is to be taught in person by a frequent user. It is our hope that this series will pique your interest in sign language.

Winter
Invierno

1.

2.

Repeat
Repita

3

Snow
Nieve

1.

2.

Snowboard
Snowboard

1.

2.

Repeat
Repita

Ice Skate
Patín de Hielo

1.

2.

Repeat
Repita

6

Ice Hockey
Hockey sobre Hielo

1.

2.

3.

Repeat
Repita

Spring
Primavera

1.

2.

Repeat
Repita

8

Bird Nest
Nido de Pájaro

1.

2.

3.

4.

9

Rain
Lluvia

1.

2.

*Repeat
Repita*

Umbrella
Paraguas

1.

2.

Summer
Verano

1.

2.

Repeat
Repita

Sunflower
Girasol

1.

2.

3.

4.

13

Bee
Abeja

1.

2.

3.

Butterfly
Mariposa

1.

2.

Repeat
Repita

15

Baseball
Béisbol

1.

2.

Repeat
Repita

Watermelon
Sandía

1.

2.

For step 2, motion
thumping a melon.
Para el paso 2, haga el gesto
de golpear un melón.

17

Fins
Aletas

1.

2.

Repeat
Repita

Ice Cream
Helado

1.

2.

**Repeat
Repita**

19

Fall
Otoño

1.

2.

Repeat
Repita

Leaf
Hoja

1.

2.

Repeat
Repita

Football
Fútbol Americano

1.

2.

Repeat
Repita

Bicycle
Bicicleta

1.

2.

Repeat
Repita

A B C D E F
G H I J K
L M N O P
Q R S T U
V W X Y Z

A SPECIAL THANK-YOU

to our models from the Program for Children Who Are Deaf and Hard of Hearing at the Alexander Graham Bell Elementary School in Chicago, Illinois:

Aroosa is in third grade in Milwaukee and loves reading, shopping, and playing with her sister Aamna. Aroosa's favorite color is red.

Carla is in fourth grade and enjoys art, as well as all kinds of sports.

Deandre likes playing football and watching NFL games on television. He also looks forward to going to the movies with his family.

Destiny enjoys music and dancing. She especially likes learning new things and spends much of her time practicing her cursive handwriting.

Xiomara loves fashion, clothes, and jewelry. She also enjoys music and dancing. Xiomara's favorite animal is the cat.